"Henrietta Goodman's is a poetry of testamen mosaic of shards and sorrows, a symphony w innocence and experience, whose cinematic cro provides evidence of a wise spirit bruised yet irrepressible. *Antillia* gestures toward a taxing history of embodied travails, of ice apples, and ghosts, a lived terrain where Goodman sees 'everything/trying to divide yet stay attached/at the root.' Here's a voice gritty, delicate, resilient, raw, a speaker with a handsaw who's 'no one's wife and no one's martyr,' instead 'a gasping head on a platter/of water' whose eyes cast floodlights on the 'Forty billion poison gallons/the geese see from air and mistake for a safe place.' Savvy to feel gifted when the "ground is finally thawed enough to bury the dead"; brilliant to define 'Happiness: the underside of a dried starfish,' Goodman reminds us that a child can be 'made of nothing,' and that a single word can birth a shattered world of loss and misunderstanding in which we nevertheless abide."

—KATRINA ROBERTS, author of *Likeness*

"Henrietta Goodman's *Antillia* is a collection of searching lyric poems that remember, joke, free associate, interrogate, worry, and examine the roots of words in pursuit of sense or solace. The world depicted is one of potential chaos and harm, though a quest for love, joy, and understanding has not been abandoned. In one Proustian meditation, the smell of Windex conjures memories of the speaker's grade school crush, yet further consideration yields recollections of a Cold War-era bomb shelter. The bewildered (or sardonic) speaker asks, 'Windex leads to Martin leads to beauty leads to bomb?' The volume's title suggests that a new world might be accessed, though at present it's more myth than fact. These aesthetically impressive poems stun with their vigor, candor, and wit."

—CHRISTOPHER BREAN MURRAY, author of *Black Observatory: Poems*

"'In the South, everything bites / and f*cks and pretends not to,' Henrietta Goodman writes in one of her trademark poems that are alive and daring and nervy: all heart and smarts, no pretense. We're so fortunate to have this new book, which moves from lovers to sons to metaphorical-real lakes to a fancy cowboy bar's 'ropes / of neon acrylic squeezed straight from the tube' to fine art to stinging truths—insisting on loving and facing head-on a world that keeps failing and falling."

—ALEXANDRA TEAGUE, author of *Or What We'll Call Desire*

The Backwaters Prize in Poetry
Honorable Mention

ANTILLIA

Henrietta Goodman

THE BACKWATERS PRESS
An imprint of the University of Nebraska Press

Acknowledgments for the use of copyrighted material appear on page 81, which constitutes an extension of the copyright page.

 The Backwaters Press is an imprint of the University of Nebraska Press.

Library of Congress Cataloging-in-Publication Data
Names: Goodman, Henrietta, 1970– author.
Title: Antillia / Henrietta Goodman.
Description: Lincoln NE: The Backwaters Press, 2024.
Identifiers: LCCN 2023029702
ISBN 9781496236081 (paperback)
ISBN 9781496239044 (epub)
ISBN 9781496239051 (pdf)
Subjects: BISAC: POETRY /
American / General | LCGFT: Poetry.
Classification: LCC PS3607.0568 A8 2024
DDC 811/.6—dc23/eng/20230626
LC record available at https://lccn.loc.gov/2023029702

Set and designed in Fanwood Text by N. Putens.

CONTENTS

ANTILLIA

1

The Puppy and Kitten Channel

Remember the night I passed my test
and the Thai place where you took me
brought my rice pressed into the shape
of a heart, a maraschino cherry bleeding
sweetly on the top? It's an old story—
once there was an atom who wanted to
be a molecule. I've thought a lot about
innocence since then—the sleeping otters
floating on their backs in the aquarium
pool, paws linked, the human presence
behind the animal videos on the Internet—
intimate laughter, murmured words
in Russian or Norwegian while puppies
lick each other's faces or a baby deer
eats from someone's hand. I've watched
the puppy and kitten channel. At the Origami
Club, you can learn to make a whole paper
world—origami strawberry shortcake,
origami water bug, origami chicken
hatching from an egg. *Do you ever feel*
completely ruined? The man with no arms
and no legs takes an egg into his mouth
and drops it into a bowl, takes a whisk
into his mouth and scrambles, takes
the bowl into his mouth and wheels
to the stove, takes a spatula into his mouth
and lifts the egg onto a plate, bits
of shell and all. Takes a fork into his
mouth. Turns and grins. *Do you feel*

ruined now? Yes, still ruined, and guilty.
Click again, and a couple laughs as a kitten
and a bunny tumble across a flowered
rug. The otters float apart, then back
together. The origami bride smooths
a wrinkle in her immaculate dress.

What Are We Going to Turn Into?

When he was four or five, my son would sometimes ask.
As if these bodies were not our final form. As if nature
or magic might deliver us. Too shy to sing at the Christmas
concert, to clap or shape his fingers into antlers or falling
snow, his hair a blond wave like Hermey the Elf's. When
one of my professors told me the only neighborhood I could
afford wasn't safe, he meant it wasn't white. I stepped
barefoot onto the porch to call my son for dinner and the door
locked behind me. My neighbors came home, and while
I gestured, not knowing how to say *locked out* or anything
else in Spanish, the man put down his groceries, crossed
my yard, removed the AC unit from my window, picked up
my son and boosted him through. I stood there repeating
gracias. I thought the people on that street might not want
us there—and they passed plates of burgers and potato salad
and chocolate cake over the fence, and Ivan's mother told him
to give the toys he had outgrown to my son—so many dinosaurs—
and I know I wasn't anything but lucky, but even the desperate
man who knocked on my door at 2:00 a.m. to try to sell a pair
of boots apologized for waking me and didn't punch through
the window. I wish I could say that when Jeremiah's grandmother
came down the street and put out her hand, I wasn't so aware
of mine—so soft, so small, so white. Almost ten years gone
from Lubbock, and last night my son brought from his father's
house a green caterpillar his father threw on an anthill. My son
reached for it, swatted the ants that climbed his arm, made it
a home with dirt and pink blossoms and leaves and sticks
in a plastic cup labeled St. Patrick's Hospital from the week

he spent there trying not to want to die, and I'm thinking
of how Gabriel's father used to go around shirtless with huge
muscles and a huge grin calling my son Casper, how we laughed
together, and I'm thinking about that question, based on
the simplest metaphor I know, the only one that matters.

Gretel Returns

Turns out Merlin is named for the bird
not the wizard. Not the Matter of Britain
but the Matter of Last Place to Get Gas,
Last Place to Call the Man who Broke
Your Heart or Anyone Else. All along,
esmerillon, not *myrddin*, and no connection
between. In the Matter of Coming Back
to Do It Better, Merlin's a little larger
now, still mostly fly shops and the Dollar
General, mostly heirloom apple trees
and one intersection where the road
finds the river. After that, Indian Mary,
Galice, then Rand and Argo and the Grave
Creek bridge, where I turn and go up.
Now the cabin has a party line walkie-talkie
phone that sometimes works, so you can
tell me again how I am tough, even when
you aren't sure it's me—a strange number
on a Thursday morning and you twenty
hours and three states away. Tell me
how you know, when you know me so
little my voice is a surprise each time.
Truly, you don't sound so tough yourself.
You sound afraid. The things I love best
here are the most fragile—not the bears,
fewer than there were, not the merlin—
bird that steals nests, eats other birds,
chases its prey up the sky. When I think
of *esmerillon*, I think of *esmé: beloved*,

though there's no connection. So tell me,
when a tree's across the road a half mile
from the cabin and it's late and I'm lucky
not to be farther out on this shattered
road crossed with snails, their wine-dark
bodies stretched smooth as the new skin
of the madrones. Tell me, when I'm
crying too hard to drive because my son
is three years gone but not gone, the way
the gone go—into the shuffle of madrone
leaves, the ferns, the hummingbirds,
the wasps, the snake with black and white
rings, purple asters, tanager blushing
like a peach. Tell me, when my tire
goes flat on a hill, when the phone
is down and the ghost of my dog Charlie
is running out at dawn to scare the crows,
when the ghost of my son is sitting
on the counter kicking his heels. Or better,
go back and tell that terrified woman
squinting into the sun, child in her arms,
wrinkles just starting around her eyes.
Tell me now, when I'm blocking
the tires with rocks, cranking the jack,
balancing the spare on my feet to fit it
onto the wheel, when I'm sawing the tree
with a handsaw in a cloud of mosquitos,
the woods creaking and snapping
and singing around me, when I think
of my beloveds, gone and everywhere.

Ice Apples

Were you a real apple once? I mean decades
ago, as a little boy in plaid flannel eating
peanuts in that faded picture. By ice apple,
I mean a mold with no cast. In those orchards
in the frozen Midwest, or on the unpruned tree
in your backyard, mined by worms, slurped
by bees, they shriveled, then froze and fell,
leaving ice globes hanging like ornaments.
You ran an ad and the gleaners came and raked
the ground to feed pigs, or maybe boil
into a not-quite-spoiled sauce. That was me,
gleaning in the aftermath of your season's
end. That summer night we drank ice wine
at your mother's house, we were sitting,
you said, on the Eastern Continental Divide.
You dribbled a little watered-down wine
off the porch, said if you poured your glass
out the front door, it would flow to the Atlantic,
and out the back, to the Pacific. There on Ridge
Avenue above the former swamp, above
the confused river flowing backward forever
now, there on the North Shore, you weren't
even right about which divide you grew up on—
the Saint Lawrence River Divide, not the Eastern
Continental. There are more divides than you
knew, and the one your mother still straddles
is mostly obsolete and has been since the reversal
of the Chicago River, and the wine you poured
out the front would have flowed to the Gulf

of Mexico, and out the back, to the Labrador Sea.
One more on the long list of things that made you
special, that and having sex with John Cusack's
little sister—I know, not Joan, the other one.
The position? Reverse cowgirl. Location?
That house on the divide, or was it at the lake,
on the dock, in plain sight? On your list
of things that made you special, that and being
what? That and being.

Asked to Imagine the Death of My Son

It's true I don't want to think of choosing
clothes in which to bury him, not just because
my son would rather burn. I'd wrap him
in a sheet and keep the clothes that hold
the damp machine smell of his sweat like oiled
gears, the cologne his first girlfriend gave him.
When my first love died, his mother dressed
him in a black suit and skinny crocheted tie
he might have liked, makeup to hide whatever
hanging does, though he would have worn
more eyeliner. My friend buried her baby
in a Montana winter twenty years ago,
a bundle small as a cat. I've buried only
an actual cat, my son's—bad enough
and my fault, since by the time we went
to the vet, it was too late. I sat on the kitchen
floor, slit the black plastic, wrapped the body
in the *Where the Wild Things Are* shirt
my son picked out. On the way to the beach
last summer, my son joked about killing someone,
and my mother said *why do you have to talk
about death all the time?* and my son said
it's a fact of life, and my mother said *why can't
you talk about other facts of life?* and I said
he talks about sex a lot, too. When my son
was six, in the cemetery where I used to sit
with my first love—my son's thumbnails
painted black, hair hanging over his eyes—
we posed for a picture. So there's my son

standing like a boy who is dead, and here he is
in the kitchen, teaching me the swing dance
moves he learned in gym—the tornado,
the pretzel, and one called the eternal spin
of death—at fourteen, an inch taller than I am,
holding me in a dip over the dirty black
and white tiles, and not dropping me.

Self-Portrait, 1921, Alberto Giacometti

The body in action fills the frame.
A green rain boot. A ship's wheel.
The body an extension of the mind,
an incarnation rolling through space.
A shimmer of color as though encased
in a soap bubble. The floor a solstice
sunrise. An ache in the jaw. Red hands,
pale wrists. A hundred years used to be
longer. Is he appraising himself, braced
against the wind? Or opening a door
at the calm center of a storm? It matters,
doesn't it, if what's on the canvas
is his own insomniac eye, or if he's
trying, across a life, to get you right?

Lake of Delight

Ship in a bottle, V of geese—nearly
neon arrow lit from underneath by
city light, snow light—the espresso's foam
a cinnamon-freckled flower, yard gnome,
the god from the machine, shift freedom key,
solitude of the ski lift, the body
naked in hot sand, northern lights, the curve
of Independence Boulevard above
the crappy town you came from, *Can't Hardly*
Wait on the radio, and yes, baby
animals, and the lock on the bridge, picked
by luck and sunk as bones. The way you kick
toward air and float. The amaretto scent
of lilies on a lake of black basalt.

Self-Portrait Playing Tennis

When we play tennis, my lover says I look
happy. I never stop chasing balls. Enthusiastic
and bumbling as a dog, I watch his high serve
and I swing and it's a strike again. The ball
bounces off the fence. It's good we're fenced in.
Another couple hits the ball long and low, on
and on. There's not much to say about that kind
of tennis. In the Girl Scouts, I ate Goldfish crackers
at the country club and learned to serve. Later,
in high school, my friends and I looped through
the drive and honked the horn long and loud, on
and on. There's not much to say about reverse
snobbery, but it's fun to annoy the rich. You
shake hands with the racket. But what do Southern
girls know about shaking hands? I moved west,
and taught my son not to squeeze if a girl
is wearing rings. The social hug, too, I learned
on my own—the little pat, only shoulders touching.
Before, I knew just two kinds—mother-daughter
or full-body, the way I hug my lover. I didn't hold
a girl's hand until I was twenty-two. Fingers laced together,
we clomped down the street in tall boots, both
in love with the same man, and oh, her hand
was soft and small, and she was hard to hate
after that. Here on the court, I shake hands
with the racket, line my fingers up, serve
and return—overhand, underhand, forehand,
backhand—why all the slapping and deception?
Never mind keeping score—we're doing well

just to get the ball across the net. The origin
of love is *l'oeuf*, the egg, or *l'heure*, the hour,
or *iets voor lof doen*, for praise instead of money.
No matter what, it's love to love at first, when—
my lover says—we send in our *representatives*.
It's easy to be on your best behavior when nothing
can hurt you. Who cares if he drinks a six-pack
every night and sleeps past noon? Who cares
if his gums bleed? It's not like you're going
to marry him. It's fun to write the word *love*, loopy,
the way we feel at the beginning, but this is not
the beginning anymore, not even close. My lover
knows my fear of death, my distaste for proverbs.
He puts on the accent of my father, whom
he never met, and tells my son *buy low,*
sell high, Scotty, and the awful one about the cow.
He knows how the word *serendipity* reminds me
of the sad festival in the park, never serendipitous,
always my mother and me alone at the art booth
where my small thumb was inked, its print doodled
into a cat or a mouse. This, though, this tennis match
in the spring sun, is what it should have meant.

Self-Portrait with Emergency Landing

Her favorite line was, *where are you going*
when you're dead? It put him on the spot,
but it was sweet when he had no answer.
She thought he'd have an answer
for everything—that was what she liked,
how with him serial killer movies
didn't scare her, her own past didn't
scare her, death didn't scare her—
that night over Wyoming, snow like arrows
aimed at the plane, ellipses previewing
the empty space of her absence, snow
like tiny white birds, no lights below,
snow like a crying baby, like a ringing
phone—but how to answer it?

Futures

Then, I only thought of the present—
his little rented house, sandalwood
incense, the heater we hovered over
at 2:00 a.m., blankets on the windows,
Gipsy Kings on the stereo. In bed
he said *you're in love with me, aren't*
you? and when I said yes, he said
without apology, *I don't feel the same.*
January, it was cold, we were lonely—
he liked me enough for that. One
afternoon we drove through a blizzard
to a bar by the highway where a single
purple betta, like an iris, charged
its smoke-blurred tank again and again.
When he was Hamlet for Halloween,
I recited to impress him: *Oh, that this*
too too solid flesh should melt, thaw,
and resolve itself into a dew. But is it
solid or *sullied*? *A dew* or *adieu*?
For my birthday that year, I made
a hazelnut torte. I could have called
it a filbert cake, but *filbert* is red-faced,
spittle-lipped, named for a monk
robed in a brown husk, shell and skin
like a caul. Years later I left my husband
and baby at home to meet him in a diner.
His voice, unchanged, his arm next to
a plate of eggs. I would have left
with him, not because I loved him then

or before or more than any other. Just
that with him I was another me. One
late night, we found an envelope
in the snow and opened it—a letter
on thin blue paper, its characters unreadable.
What did we do with it? So many years,
I've wondered what it said, why it seems
so easy and so impossible to put back.

The Man behind the Curtain

Who is the man behind the curtain?
My ex-husband likes to think it's him,
likes to use phrases like *the elephant*
in the room, which is the opposite,
or is it? He's no elephant, either,
not with that turkey neck—no rock
star with a guitar over his shoulder
and all those lovely girls, cheeks
dusted with glitter. Master of cliché
and crocodile tears, why couldn't he
be an elephant behind the curtain,
or even better, just a man in the room?
Now he's balding in a lavender tie,
vice president of something IT, talking
to a curator of Asian Arts (*Oriental*,
my mother would say) at the most boring
party ever. Twenty years back, at the Shag
House, Merle Haggard's on the stereo
and a guy's tearing sides of salmon
into chunks for the grill, eating raw
bits behind a curtain of smoke—
he's loaded, they say, and they don't
mean rich. He has goat eyes—one
wanders, literally. Which would you
rather have—betrayal or lazy eye?
Do you play *would you rather?*
The man in the tie says *I saw it*
in the ocean, meaning some kind
of tiny shrimp, white as a cave-fish,

maybe also that image from Qi Baishi's
ink wash. The rocks roll back and roll
back, like someone racking the balls
at a pool table. A curtain of water
falls from a cliff over the beach,
and behind it, just trees covered in moss
or lichen, leaves and vines. Hot vanilla
milk was a thing once, before bed
on Friday night after moo goo gai pan
or egg fu yung at the *Oriental* restaurant,
my mother remembering her Japanese
friend interned during the war, and her
friend's father too. *Mama tried.* I mean,
I guess she did. She wouldn't know
the song, though. Truly, there's no one
back there controlling any of this—
the past, the future, the words we use
to defend, or forgive.

Lake of Winter (Berryman)

Those videos made soon before his death—
so drunk his voice is mush and stagger. You
can hear the needle ice, the mud, frost heaves,
the rime and slush, the ice-jacked fracturing
of girders. An afterthought, the jump. Here,
the edge of sleep, a shape appears, less dream
than apprehension—bearded, featureless,
transparent, seated in a chair—the smell
of whiskey and the outline of a man
filled with a swarm of screws and nuts and bolts,
bright steel, unstuck. He could be anyone,
this human Cornell box, this scrambled bin
of hardware. But you see through him to him—
the frozen surface, dark flash of a fin.

Self-Portrait as a Stranger

Who is that girl you see across the pool,
her skin a winter cloud in hot springs'
steam? At first you think her distant
as the elk that cross the ridge above
the lodge, slender in the knee and hoof,
stopped motionless to test the wind.
Her wet hair curves, a leather cap.
The strings of her bikini hang, a quiver
of arrows at her thigh. Some girls
would rather hunt than love. From
where you drift along the concrete wall,
the hottest jet pounding your back,
wine blood-warm in your paper cup,
all that should be soft is sharp—
her wet-spiked lashes, double
helix of her hipbone's jut and twist,
lemniscate that cuts the edge
of silhouette. Her gaze confronts
the ridge, a gaze that you imagine
bruised and bruising what it sees—
certain it would burn like this water
on cold skin, the feverish thump
of heated blood. But when she turns,
the yellow tamaracks behind her lit
by evening sun, and shivers as wind
stirs the steam, with what measure
of disappointment and relief
do you distinguish—mine, the open
hands, the strange, familiar mouth?

Caryatids

On the table, coffee, a small pitcher of syrup,
silverware wrapped like mummies, or virgins.
While the crowd across the patio argues Chevy
versus Ford over Bloody Marys and mimosas,
we're deciding whether to be Plath and Hughes
or Bishop and Lowell—quietly, because like
the sugar, we're refined, or you are. I'm more
the kind in the brown packet, raw, turbinado,
a tornado. At least we're not that counterfeit
pastel rainbow: pink saccharine, blue aspartame,
yellow sucralose. You know the white is over-
processed, a waste of energy, right? But fine,
for you I'll say *fuck* in public a little more
softly. Sylvia bit his cheek the night they met,
but that's not what you meant, is it, when you
said you want me for your poetry? You didn't
mean a muse, either—a muse is just furniture,
or décor, like Plath's caryatids in the piece
by Robus. To hold your head up with no portico
pressing down, that's everyone's dream. No
caryatids here, just a gargoyle, or maybe
a grotesque, high on the side of the building.
The neck of a caryatid is the most fragile—
thus, the elaborate hair woven into a broad
paddle, like a leaf. You meant like Lowell
and Bishop, less drama, more Scrabble, no one
throwing a drink or going after the other
with a butter knife. Once I threw a glass past
a man's head, aiming for the flagstone behind

him. At worst, he got sprayed with water
like a bad cat. I wanted the sound of shattering—
hard and fragile meeting hard and tough, the way
a diamond cuts glass. Who would I break against,
or who would break against me? Later, he insisted
I had thrown it *at* him but in addition to all
my other flaws, my aim was bad. Sometimes
I want to be the diamond, sometimes the glass.
At the Acropolis, the caryatids are cleaned
with a laser. It's like a facelift. Less harmful
than touching. I suppose they're used to being
hovered over, like reiki. Like sex with a ghost.
And then there's hostile architecture—that bench
interrupted by armrests, spikes embedded
in doorways, so you can't sit out of the rain.
A body too can be designed to discourage
anyone from getting comfortable. That's what
happens when you mistake tears for rhetoric—
you can't comfort me. But guerrilla troops are
traveling city streets and parks with wrenches,
removing the bolts and bars to let people lie down.

I Want To Be a Door

> I wanna, I wanna, I wanna, I wanna be adored.
> —THE STONE ROSES

His compliment: *you look adorable.* Meaning,
I could be adored, but not necessarily by him.
Meaning I am not necessarily adorable,
but I look like I might be. Meaning I am small
and harmless. *What an adorable otter-print*
purse. What an adorable toddler toddling
through the saloon in a daisy dress. To call
someone likeable is not to say you like them.
To say that road is drivable or that car is drivable
is not to mean you will do any driving. To say
I adore you is, at least, to own a romantic
or religious feeling, yet even that means less
than it used to. One might say *I adore Jesus,*
but not *Jesus is adorable,* unless one means
the baby in his straw cradle, but probably not
even then. *Adore* has weakened, as with
awesome, which now means, basically, *ok.*
So now I'm running with that stupid song
stuck in my head, face stung by June sleet,
meadowlarks calling. What I know: any man
who wants to be adored by one woman wants
to be adored by all, meaning not really seen
by any, which is why that song is about the devil,
who is less sexy than he used to be. Maybe,
instead, you could want to be a door. Maybe you
see me that way already, since you come

in me, but I mean more in a Robert Duncan
kind of way, a passage, *a hall therein*. If you'll
be a door for me, I'll be a door for you,
and together we'll go in and out, not like sex
or fast food, not the way a camera narrows
and freezes infinite space, not a frame around
a portion of these snowy mountains, but more
the way mist over water parts, then gathers,
then parts again. You can't stay closed forever.
You can't stay the same, like the bad cowboy art
in the respectable bar where we take out-of-towners
until we learn whether they'd like the dive bar
better—or must we stay there, under those ropes
of neon acrylic squeezed straight from the tube?

Opossum of the Month

Would you like to join the Opossum
of the Month Club? I wake with this
in mind, a bar of TV-light under the door—
my nocturnal love out on the couch
in his Xtratuf ball cap binge-watching
some show, too sober to sleep. The characters
are going back in time, moving into new
bodies. One of my students wants to study
the *science* of reincarnation, and I keep
explaining there's no peer-reviewed research
into how a soul enters a body like a Porta-Potty
and flips the sign from vacant to occupied.
It's better than suicide of the month,
depressed alcoholic of the month.
I'm dumb enough to wonder, still,
what combination of hummingbirds
and pills might help. The opossum
can have twenty-five babies and play dead for hours,
drooling, eyes fixed. Immune to rattlesnake
venom, it acts tough but isn't. I saw one
in North Carolina years ago at least once
a month on the chainlink fence under the full
moon—maybe more than one, since they
don't live long, but how would I know,
when they're all so much the same?

Sea of Desire

> There was also a region on the Lunar farside that was
> briefly misidentified as a mare and named *Mare Desiderii*
> (Sea of Desire). It is no longer recognized.
>
> —LIST OF MARIA ON THE MOON, WIKIPEDIA

What it's not is complicated. Of course none of them are real lakes—
only desire turns a depression into wetness, a navigable body.
But this lake named and then unnamed reminds you of the way
thyme spreads between flagstones, or the woman at the pool
in the black two-piece, seventy at least, her body traced with ink
faded to mossy-green—shapes and names like wet leaves
or lakeweed, veins or bruises. Or that picture from twenty years
ago of a man in a doorway threading your earring through the eye
of your earlobe—why? You don't remember. What you remember is
he didn't touch you, just the thin silver hook that in that moment
he twists to find the smoothest passage. You saw a man do it
to your friend a few years ago in a bar in Seattle. On her face
the same expression. She had a husband, this man was not
her husband, they had just met and would never meet again.

Free Association

> Free associating, that is to say, is akin to mourning; it is a
> process of detachment that releases hidden energies.
> —ADAM PHILLIPS

Always the smell of Windex brings me back to Martin Shelton
in first grade, his memory atomized from some forgotten source.
It's wind and window when I see him late for school through double
doors of tempered glass, then rushing in on the lovely trochaic
feet of his name, shirt buttoned wrong, blond hair blown in a gust
of oak leaves, smoke, and frost that swept away the simmered meat
and rubber smells, the green litter that soaked up accidents. The wind
recorded and erased. I was afraid to sit with him, or speak—
my first crush a boy who packed his own lunch and walked alone
through dark stairwells hung with Bomb Shelter signs, arrows
aimed at the basement lunchroom where we bowed our heads
to wait for fallout's drift from the split atom, the invisible anvil
that could fall no matter where we hid. Even when the speakers
hummed and Mr. Wells announced that we were safe,
his name said the earth would swallow us. And now I spray
the glass to wipe away the prints, the trace, but traces gone,
the glass I see through stays. How, then, could mourning set me free,
if Windex leads to Martin leads to beauty leads to bomb?

Antillia

Sick with the kind of fever that makes you grateful
for everything, I asked for the *Moonlight Sonata*
and he put it on and I lay on the couch and drank
orange pineapple mango juice, which was the best
juice ever, even though it was just Dole and not
organic and from a plastic-lined cardboard carton
probably leaking pthalates. I couldn't taste them.
I lay there with tears dripping into my ears saying
it's so beautiful while he made coffee and toast
with honey. It's easy to fall in love with heat
when you have a fever and believe you're freezing.
The same with hypothermia, when you're so cold
you start to burn, and strew your clothes over the snow
as though death is a bedroom you're swept into
by a passion so strong you don't care what thread
and buttons you scatter behind. Why is even
temperature so unreliable? And why was that bird
in his yard a *lesser* goldfinch, when it was perfectly
yellow and lovely? And why are the Antilles
lesser? Aren't they really less than lesser,
since Antillia doesn't exist and never did—
like the Fortunate Islands, the Isles of the Blest?
Antillia means *island of the other* or *opposite island*
or *the inaccessible*, meaning, of course, you, or
hell is other people, or, as it was meant, *hell is*
the otherness of people, meaning not the individual
you—don't worry, I'm not writing about *you*—
you don't exist except as a phantom island, sorry.
If I were a bird, I might be the lesser Henrietta

but at least not the least. Though if you judged
my worth based on how little you had to work
to have me, you might understandably call me so.
To be just given something of value—like the car
my ex-husband's parents gave him after he drove
his off a cliff. The idea that someone might give me
a car I didn't have to work for all year in a greasy
fried chicken place—if I had known, all along,
that it was so easy. I felt duped. It's different
kinds of work—to obtain, to sustain, to validate,
like parking. To keep my bad opinions to myself.
It was knapweed honey, that morning, from a noxious
weed whose roots displace the native nectar-producing
blooms, diminishing the realm of the bees,
while the bees make the sweetest, clearest honey.

Lake of Death

At the drive-up coffee shop, one of the flavors
is *stone fruit*, and we argue over whether stone
fruit is one single fruit or a category. I'm saying
peaches, plums, nectarines, cherries, but I'm thinking
of stone as a unit of measure, and the weight
of a body, and *stone cold dead*, and the obvious
difference between a seed and a stone, between
a seed and death. Another word for stone fruit
is *drupe*, which sounds like *dupe*, and some berries
are not actually berries. The thimbleberry—
made of drupelets, which sounds like *droplets*,
like a cross between a raspberry and bread,
like a blood-covered thimble from a fairy tale,
but thimbleberries have no thorns, and a thimble
covers the finger, so where does the blood
come from? Even that's a trick. Each drupelet
a tiny stone fruit, little drop of flesh around a stone,
a bone, a seed. Little drops falling into nothingness.
Little parts of a whole, singular and not.

Postcolonial Melancholia

> The way downward is easy . . . But to retrace your steps to heaven's air, There is the trouble.
> —*THE AENEID* 6.187–90

At first it didn't feel like falling. More
like being caught in a pair of talons
and shaken, hard. In American Falls,
I read *Midnight's Children* in a cold
room off the hanger while he repaired
the plane. Flying home, we traced
the Snake River, then the Salmon—
River of No Return, turbulence jolting
us north. Based on the name, you might
think the worst of that current-carved
tunnel of black-green water, might
assume it's a metaphor for time, not
just a river too steep and rocky to run
upstream until Glen Wooldridge made
it look easy in 1948. Over the river,
a hawk—*accipiter*—from *accipere,*
to grasp, to seize, but how did it come
also to mean *accept,* as a gift? *Accipiter*
once meant, too, *a rapacious man—*
plundering, greedy. From Latin, like
rape and *rapt* and *rapture* and *raptor.*
From *rapio—to grab, snatch, carry off,*
and there is, of course, what *snatch*
means as a noun. *Rape* once meant
to transport with delight. And other

obsolete definitions—*rapt: to carry*
away by force, or *an abducted woman*,
or *raped* or *taken away by death*.
Later, *rapt* became only metaphoric
transport: *to carry away in spirit*, or
deeply absorbed or buried in—so death
became metaphor, too. For Christians,
the transport of believers to Heaven,
though motion, not the end of motion,
best consoles: the way a child asleep
on the seat of a car resists being carried
to bed. Rapt now: *transported by joy*,
delight, or *a trance, ecstasy, rapture*.
Rapture of the deep: by most accounts,
a seductive death. A person cannot,
it seems, *choose* to be rapt any more
than one could choose to be raped.
So *rape* and *rapt* split based not
on choice but enjoyment. That night
in American Falls, we played *Straight*
to Hell on the jukebox, made out across
the space between barstools. How
does an American fall? Like the river,
clear as winter ice? Or is what looks
like falling an eagle's stoop toward prey,
wings pulled in, tilted horizontal,
like the plane in a deliberate slip.

Red-Winged Blackbirds

You think he's taken you to an ordinary place? A little park behind a strip mall,
cattails in late spring—dingy fluff like stuffing bursting through the threadbare
upholstery of some abandoned couch, spilling down the stalks like foam
on a glass. Trampled dirt, bedraggled grass, a few candy wrappers, turtles
sunning on logs. You know him just well enough to fight—and why

are you so afraid of loving someone who will die? Canada geese swim toward
your empty hand, expecting bread, and then you see the first red-winged
blackbird, then another, then four, quadrupling what you thought was singular,
rare—the air and trees are full of them—a trick of nature, to withhold

or give too much. A creek links two shallow ponds with a trail between them
and around, a figure eight, the shape of infinity, but the stream runs in
on one end, out on the other—that's how it is. Does he not know the red blaze
on these birds' wings is the same as the red bill of the black swan that sailed

across the cemetery pond, its wake trailing like a veil? Does he not know the bill
of that swan is the red lipstick on the lips of the first boy you ever loved,
and the graceful neck of that swan is his neck wrapped in rope—how he stepped
out of the tree, eighteen years old, and dropped? How would he know?
There are too many of them, these beauties, this darkness with a slash of red.

2

I Don't Require Durability in a Swan

An inappropriate cowboy hat, and that look—
the hills burning, dogfights and lost children.
Every day, another. I walk at night, order bees
in the mail. We change the past each time
we tell it—that disease, that too-short skirt—
go change it. Was there ever an authentic version,
a time of no cars on the road, no men in cars,
no man masturbating at the stoplight, all the hills
burning? The clouds mammary, bruised pinks
and grays. In the South, everything bites
and fucks and pretends not to. Take this car
in the river. Take this inventory of scars.
A helicopter thumps in the distance
like the heart of a scared animal, then closer.

The manhole covers don't steam like womanholes,
and you wear clothes so tightly woven they might
as well be bulletproof. Globes of mistletoe hang
from the trees like little poison earths. Lions hang
over the branches, sleeping. The tongue of the lion
scrapes your skin. The white berries glow as dark
comes down, comes up, fills all the clear places.
Tonight, wear that suit that isn't black but the deep
blue of astronomical twilight, the shoulders built in.

And oh my god he was such an asshole, but I'm keeping this one thing, it's mine,
the way he said junkyards from the air look like sequins on a girl's sweater.

Though everything that lives above ground has been
buried, we fall back, stunned, pushed over like cows
in a field, not understanding daylight saving time,
or the purpose of unadulterated truth. The clocks
are not stopped, they are only all fucked up. You're
talking about your father sleeping in front of the TV,
his weight greater than the mystery in which you veil
yourself, but most of all how a circle became a circle—

At the first interview—*What is your vision of the future
and where do you see yourself in it?* People stand
by the road taking pictures of claw marks on the trunk,
the bear in the tree, draped over a branch three stories up
like a black sack of straw, limp eggplant, velvet curtain.
This is what I'm good at—the deliberate wearing
of clothes with holes, menswear, atavistic blazers—

She passes out garments like drinks, as pumpkins
soften and bleach in unseasonal heat. Moths?
Check. Holes? Check. Jackets grow on fences,
without interrogation. Did you know, a squirrel
will eat anything for twenty, no, twenty-five bucks.
I had a provincial revelation in the ICU—
and other things that hands do.

Blind Oscar shakes pepper into his palm, licks it,
chooses the salt—sticky table, fried chicken crumbs,
chicken parts soaking in pink salt water in gray
plastic bins. Texas Pete hot sauce and drifts of flies
on the sills and Oscar's handprint on the Styrofoam
cup of sweet tea. My mother stopped the car to pick
cotton—brown bolls splitting, the whitest white
spilling out, so white it hurt. It was quaint, a novelty,
an origin-lesson. *But what will people think?*

This is how you found me. I stayed in one place like someone lost in the woods,
in the hooting and rustling and cracking and the hollow trees and the wetness
and the dryness, the inedible berries and the indelible night. I stayed still
like someone hunting in a blind, not blind, like someone pretending to be lost.

Where does the template come from? Yellowed
plastic with a slot at the top and holes where the age
shows how it preexists everything. Insert a card
in the slot, a dance card or a calling card, obsolete—
it fits. He's smoking a cigarette in the yard, he's talking
about his father sleeping in front of the TV, cows
are sleeping in the pasture at the end of the street.
You get an extra hour here, an extra hour before
time starts up again, he's saying this, you're talking
about your father sleeping in front of the TV—

I fill the pepper grinder so he can pepper his eggs
the way my father peppered his eggs, peppercorns
bouncing on the counter like BBs, the crow lifting
with a rustle like taffeta. He's in a house with a woman
who talks like he isn't there, like nothing can be fixed
or changed—a matter of real estate, a matter of
he can't see me, of Cupid and Psyche. I walk out
the door, thinking maybe it's not too late, thinking
of the one time I turned away, on a dance floor,
certain he would follow, and he did—

The morning sun blinks horizontal through the window,
yellow on the gray interior, across your arm, your cheek,
unsteady beam, rotating flicker of minor emergency.
The sun goes to sleep like your German neighbor
at 4:30 in winter and rises late, and until then the yard
is underwater, no magpies, no cows, no crows.

Who will stand beside your car? Under the mattress,
a white candle, a feather, a key, all tied with red ribbon,
barren fields lit by fire. In this costume I nurse the baby.
I nurse a gun whose sound can hem in the moon,
my face smeared with ash. Something happens
in a square, something happens in the woods—kissed,
by warm air swirled, something called *whore's breath.*
Their legs superconducting, they dive—

Seagulls over the mountains, not lost the way
you thought—this land, adoptable. The moss
green of the creek overflows and the darkening sky,
the bison in a field, the brain in a field, a cow and a calf.
A calm. You are drenched. No. *You are drenched.*

To start with, there is none of what anyone said
or is saying now—just a mumble like water or dreams,
the neighbor's fireworks burned out, sparkler bombs
and machine gun imitators. So many nights, you
on the phone with a backdrop of bar noise like a black
velvet curtain, an oblivion, you in it, losing my voice
in the dim din of many, drifting—

It could have been, or was, the day Scotty and I built a snowman and a snowwoman
and a snowchild and dressed them, gave them hats and faces—the snow endlessly
fresh and white and perfect for building beautiful and impermanent things.
The dog catching snowballs in his mouth. The smell of woodsmoke, coffee,
eggs and bacon on the stove under a plate.

When we say what we want, we use the infinitive
because desire is infinite. He shot his friend right
in the back, but it sounds like a question, always
a question—all the good Christian trees sighing
for more beer or any damn thing. *I seen you,*

she sings, *I seen you*. She holds it like a gun, swath
of clear ground where the wires run. *In that black*
car or some other do-gooder vehicle, they don't pray
for me or any other sinner. We're all rude in this
weather. Floaters leave the river at dusk in giddy
groups, dishes clatter—a couple argues in whispers,
two children chant tunelessly until the father
says *good Christ, shut up*.

A blue wolf howls, driven as the hammer drives
at the foot of the sea, horizon spliced with wavering
crosses, the heat like a misplaced predator, water
studded with empty wooden islands. Three people
drink vodka in a car in the parking lot of Hardees,
then *are you a girl or a boy* and feet kick the door.
Memory stands beside language like luggage by a train,
and three speckled eggs, a small movement inside
the shell. Inside a bell there is no sound, the nest
abandoned by suitcases, by blue fragments.

The mosquitoes love me—frogs at the lake
like a slack string plucked, the lavender sky.
On the home tour we wore surgical booties,
saw a painting of glitter-dolphins somersaulting
through a neon blue ocean—the remains
of a man who tied a concrete block around
his waist, erased. On the clock, a girl lounges
in a martini glass, butt bobbing like an olive.
A monster must be created. The monster
must be literal. Here, it's a dry heat.

Unplanted, I was made to rise, disparate as nebulae—
Polaroid pictures, cliff-jumping. My son found
a knife open in the sand. He's in a lot of these shots,

warm breath, sunscreen, fishnet catching minnows,
pistachio shells, red apple fallen from a raft. If you
want to see, the knife's open at the edge—he almost
stepped on it. And that time I lay in bed with a man
while my son picked up a razor from the table.
How long it took me to look. How the knife came
to be open, how I said, more than once, *there's no knife.*

I'm already there—same path, same farm, same cows, same fruit. Hours watering, hours watching the quick, hunched parade of scorpions. Hours building fences and planting seeds, beyond the body's refusals, beyond the tower where bats circle in the evenings. I don't have to go back.

The wind's grim salsa over the roof, a light
like dirty water. You can know things without
knowing you know them. If we send people
to Mars, they can't come back, but they can
email. He is a wave as well as a particle,
typing into the atmosphere, out of the prison
of molecules. We judge worth by effort, unless
we have to wait too long, and then we don't.

In spring, the ice on the lake melts in black, amoebic holes.
The newborn fawn ran in front of your car before I knew you,
and the tears you said you shed are long gone too—*shed,*
as though they were in you so long they were extinct
by the time you shed them—how good to be rid of that
ugly winter coat, that flaking skin. *Whisper those sweet*
nothingnesses to me again—

Of course it's fire, I write, here with my blood pen—
that red inkblot, fingerprint, red abstraction, heavy
at the bottom, excitement at the top. The ring
contains it, garnet gripped by silver not yet thinned

by decades of communion with the hand. Not gold
or diamonds. Silver is for being discarded, sunk
in the silt. Where's the fire, people say. Can't they
see my face, criss-crossed with static? No engraving,
no initials or dates to outlast memory. Who knows
who they were, how they loved, if they loved—

Which came first, ravens or ravenous? It's a reprimand,
a teapot with a face, existential crisis of your choice,
or glasses versus contacts, French accent, memory
of your father sleeping in front of the TV. A cell phone
transforms into a baby, an eye twitch, a gun. I don't trust
anything about you—you drank my gin, left me drunk
at a bad bar. I still hear the pool balls break like loosed
planets, zippers unzipping like centipedes. You crow
about it, now, how easy it was to ravage, to ravish.

Are you cold? I'm cold and there are too
many clouds and not enough vodka,
a framed painting of a woman with no face
and a G-shaped depression in the soil.
It's not the G-spot, that crater on a moonscape.
A child screams *I don't love you*. Everyone
could be a better mother. Even you, old man.
You're not as much fun as you used to be,
and even then you weren't much fun.
The potatoes are rotting in the ground.
And the father asleep in front of the TV?
You can't be him or beat him.

In the hollow, the virgin, surely post-industrial
in her calico shawl, waits for a train to take her
from one cold place to another. It's all birth
and death out here—early lambs in the fields,

lamb in the kitchen drinking from a medicine
dropper, lambs on the graves. Mint spreads
between the stones, up through the cracks.
Deer skulls adorn a tree, bleached against
the black trunk. That madam under the mound,
turned toward the railroad, away from the rest—
even now, she knows what you want, how much
you'll pay when you come back.

3

When Frankenstein Chased His Creature across the Ice

> It's as though each one of our tears carries a microcosm of the collective human experience, like one drop of an ocean.
> —ROSE-LYNN FISHER, *THE TOPOGRAPHY OF TEARS*

When Frankenstein chased his creature across the ice,
did they each think of the ninth circle of hell, the realm
of treachery? Or were they by then one single thing,
traitor and betrayed, their pursuit a kind of ouroboros?
Or did they think, simply, of that treacherous polar
terrain, imagine it endless, unchanging? I read it
in my grandmother's house, sitting on the black bench
stuffed with hair harvested from manes and tails,
a better batting than marsh grass, which wouldn't
hold its shape. In Victorian hair art, white or gray
is horse hair—people died young. But control for
infant mortality and childhood illness and that's a myth—
if you made it to forty, you'd likely see seventy. And another
one—lachrymatory bottles weren't, after all, used
to collect tears, but to hold perfume. Useful, still,
at summer funerals. And what of those slides
categorizing crystalized tears? Grief creates
a sparse landscape, a blueprint—lines of walls
and streets, roundish spots for bushes or trees.
Laughter: melting ice cream or blown glass, psychedelic.
Happiness: the underside of a dried starfish or branching
veins, bronchioles of a lung, watercourses, plants.
Happiness must be more varied than grief. But as much
as we want to believe our tears unique as snowflakes
yet also shared, at most the fern forest of onion

tears might differ from the residue of sorrow or cold
wind. But how the tears are dried, whether the crier
was thirsty, sick, drunk, would make my grief-tear
different from yours, make even the grief-tear
I cried today different from yesterday's, or tomorrow's.
How to account for the way tears sometimes spurt
and sometimes leak as from a faucet that takes hours
to drip once, but is nonetheless never dry? Water spots
on a letter. A watermark, thinned with wire while the paper
is wet. The waterline of the eye, lined with kohl. And
waterlines on porcelain or on a hill, where a glacial lake
receded. That shelf of ice—Thwaites, the Doomsday
Glacier. How fast will the water rise if it breaks?
The ice falls into the ocean, then more slips along,
then the whole West Antarctic Sheet goes. Or, if it
just melts, a slow rise of several feet. At first. Later,
another ten. Only twenty-eight people have stood in Doomsday's
katabatic winds—arrived, maybe, on a blue ice runway
made, or exposed, by those winds rushing down to
the ocean. Katabasis: a descent in search of understanding.
Or, depression in young men. Or, a trip to the underworld.
True katabasis must be followed by anabasis, an ascent.
Otherwise, it's just death. How long does it take the mane
and tail to grow? Hair art: not just mourning jewelry,
but wreaths, dioramas housed under bell jars, made
by palette work and table work and gimp work
and the grinding of hair into pigment. Not just
memento mori, but hair of the living too.

The Men at Snowbowl Teaching Their Daughters to Ski

The first one is half a couple, young, their daughter
four or five in pink snow pants and a pink flowered
coat. They're stopped at the top of the last long run,
skis wedged sideways. She's made it this far, and now
she's wailing *I can't do it I can't do it I don't want to—*
Almost everyone pauses before this sheer slope
gleaming in late-afternoon sun, this almost-vertical
descent that someone named Paradise. She's sobbing
I can't do it and her father says *What do you need?*
Do you need some fish? Do you need some T. Swift?
He reaches for his phone and "Shake It Off" starts playing,
and he barks like a seal and flaps his arms and stomps
his skis a little like flippers, and she holds out
her gloved hand and he puts goldfish crackers in it,
tosses a few and catches them in his mouth, and they
start down Paradise, her skis in a careful pizza,
her father telling her when to turn. The next one
is older, bearded, his daughter older too, high school
or college, hard to tell through helmet and goggles—
she's silent as he coaches: *drop your shoulder, now*
shift your hips, now turn, drop your shoulder.
I'm trying to translate his advice into something
my own body could do—toes curled in my boots,
skis crossed at the tips, poles flailing behind me
and sticking in snow as I skid toward the trees.
She's making long slow turns; he's patient, saying
over and over *good girl* in a way that means she's
as frightened as I am and her goodness is his world
and is, to him, absolute. She doesn't look at him—
she's watching her skis as they glide back and forth
through Paradise, watching herself not falling.

The Petroleum Club

What if, as I first heard it, the Petroleum Club
was the Trillium Club, named for a small lily,
a birthroot unfurling its three white or pink
or deep red petals through layers of leaves
wet with snowmelt and frilled with ice?
Extraction isn't that kind of birth—it's more
like raising the dead, for money. Passing
a Sinclair station, my son, at five, asked
is gas made of dinosaurs, then *why did you
get divorced?* Then, into the sunset blooming
orange *is it the same time everywhere?* Nature.
Love. Time. He covered everything. It sank in,
then—what had I thought *fossil fuel* meant?
Death under time and pressure equals oil.
At the Petroleum Club, the top of the tallest
hotel in the state, all of eastern Montana
spreads twenty-two floors below, the occasional
pumpjack nodding like a braying donkey,
or like Pinocchio, my lover, holding
an Old-Fashioned, mouthing the liar's
paradox to his reflection—*I am a liar, this
sentence is false*—but mostly refineries
lit up like amusement parks, Pleasure Island.
In this glass room, I can't stop thinking
of a true story I'd like to forget—a child
who tumbled from a window like these,
a mother who ran all the flights to the street.
And there's the imaginary child my lover
conceived, the one I can't stop mourning now,

even though, or maybe because, it never existed
except in his detailed, appalling fabrication.
Zeus, fearing his child would be wiser
than he, swallowed his wife. Seven wives
later, head throbbing in near-uterine
contractions, he asked for his skull to be
opened with an ax and Athena emerged,
warrior armed with helmet and spear,
split from the hemispheres of his brain.
In my lover's story, the child is not fully-formed—
only the story is, since in the story, the child,
a boy, is never born. How many ways does
the word *miscarriage* apply? He loved her;
she left him, and so he imagined her death,
the child's death—a child made of nothing
but pain and his need to give it shape.
As if nothing real, not even his suffering,
was ever good enough. And so, the tableau—
a woman, pregnant, behind the wheel of a car,
windshield shattered, glass stained not with
pigment but blood. To add color to glass
is to impregnate. To make clear glass red,
add gold. The stain lasts centuries. A beam
passing through it stabs everything in its path,
a kind of stigmata—red on the flowers,
the table, the sheets, his body, my body.

Seahorse

My son throws his phone against the wall,
crushes the shattered screen to glitter
and sprinkles it on me, like rain or seeds—
where it lands, blood wells. Bad fairy dust,
cast by my son who at seven danced with me
through the solstice dark—black windows,
cold floor, every other person gone. He throws
a pan through the kitchen—glass explodes.
Once, at the ocean, a seahorse seemed to smile
at us—yellow and speckled, tail curled
like a fiddlehead fern, little translucent fin
like a fan on its back, waving. Hippocampus,
it's called, hybrid of horse and monster, the same
as the part of the brain that won't let us forget.

Organizational Systems

Some homework—phylum: chordata.
Nerve cord. Spinal cord. Chords played
on the guitar by the neighbors' daughter
one summer night years ago. *Chord*
from French for *accord*, or just *cord*:
a string. No difference, really, but spelling.
Vascular plants: coniferophyta. Phloem,
xylem. The way sap rises. Country music—
alt-country, classic, traditional, bluegrass,
punkgrass. Angiospermaphyta: grasses.
What we might agree on: maybe Hank
Williams. *I'm So Lonesome I Could Cry*.
Little else. But years of pears passed
over the fence, raspberries, tomatoes,
peppers. Years of summer evenings,
the blades of a mower cutting blades
of grass. Children's voices, small bodies
splashing in the small pool, the neighbor's
laugh—deep, bubbling up from the bottom
of the ocean—how can I say that even
after what her son did to my son, her
laugh through open windows still means
summer? The cherry tree splitting in two,
the spruce splitting in two, everything
trying to divide yet stay attached
at the root, her daughter leaving home,
my son never leaving his room, the way
words can be both nouns and verbs—
the split, to split, the splinter, to splinter,

the touch, to touch—what her son did
to my son in a basement room when
my son was eight and her son was eleven.
What I didn't know for years. What I never
told her. When her son was ten he did
a perfect Lady Gaga in our garage—
was it "Bad Romance" or "Poker Face"?
It wasn't "Born This Way," which I suddenly
saw he was. Daniel, whom I had known
since before my son was born. And what
would it mean for him? His life a lion's den.
And what does it mean for my son? *Molest*
can be a noun too, meaning *trouble,*
injury. One can be molested by doubts
and suspicions, by gout or headaches.
Or by a neighbor who is also a child,
but older. A splinter of glass from
the garage window slid under the skin
of my arm—three years later emerged
and left a little arrow scar, a beak
like the mouth of a bird or a shark,
or was it a lion? What, after that, was not
a lion? I dreamed my son took off his skin
and entered another body. He opened
his mouth—a lion, my son, maybe also
Daniel, and I was afraid, though I don't
know whether of him or for him. I knew
him by his teeth, bared, bare—not a roar
or a laugh. A silence, opening wider.

Self-Portrait in the Blackfoot

What we are left with is the fact that every organism
wishes to die only in its own fashion.
—SIGMUND FREUD, *BEYOND THE PLEASURE PRINCIPLE*

Between the beach where someone else's children
splash knee-deep and the cliffs where the brave
or drunk jump, the current tugs me out, then eddies
back toward its source—an orange slug-track oozing
through mine tailings, a field of stinging nettles
and a door in a hill, timber-framed and black.
You'd never know it here, where the fishing, rafting,
tubing crowds put in or out and the moss-green
water tumbles clean and cold. Here, the river refuses
to lose its name through its own mouth ten miles
downstream. The river wants to die in its own
way, and wants company—the little girl in the blue
bikini drifts into the deep channel, stretches her toes,
touches nothing, and begins to flail. I take her arm
and kick toward shore but when she grabs and clings,
I go down, her hands on my head. I'm under long
enough to circle past the day I stood on an edge
of sun-baked rock and my son yelled *jump and I'll*
think you're cool forever, past the night I waded out
in my wedding dress, my new husband drunk and mad.
An arm grabs the girl and hauls her in, and I'm light
enough to float again—a gasping head on a platter
of water—no one's wife and no one's martyr.

Self-Portrait with Northern Lights

Static cracks in the folds of the blanket
as they tip their heads together, certain
this display of green light that billows
like a tree and twists in wild tendrils
means nature approves. Eden needs
retrospect—otherwise, why would she
cast herself out into this night, naked,
the sky like rippling neon curtains
she doesn't really want to see through?
Already, she knows innocence toughens
not to knowledge but a willful ignorance
that chokes the whole garden. In high school,
aproned and goggled, she pressed a scalpel
to the belly of a formaldehyde-drenched
cat, skin taut under the vinegary fur,
and couldn't press farther without naming
the body God. It went over badly. It's all
like high school, still—his giddy grin when
he brings the kind of coffee she likes,
the ease with which he unsnaps
her stocking—where did he learn that?—
on a bare mattress in his basement
apartment, flaking pans left on the stove,
thick cords crossing the floor, guitar
to amp to stereo, pulsing with visible
sound. And her rented room where
the manager knocks and demands a dollar
if her guest is staying the night—before
they decide, even, they begin to pay.

Self-Portrait with Seven Fingers (Marc Chagall, 1912)

Marc Chagall, why so assiduous? My father
was a Russian Jew like you. Provincial,
autodidactic, he roasted potatoes
over fires in the gutters of Manhattan,
read Shakespeare in a leather armchair.
Look at my nose, this bulb, red as borscht,
it's his, and the pawn shops where my mother
held me by the hand while she sold
her rings, and the deli with the dusty jars
of gefilte fish, the pennies, the plastic bank,
they're all his, and the polyester Santa suit—
who was he trying to fool? And you,
who turned your hand into that boxing mitt
of many colors, who made you the cat
with extra claws? A spot of red runs round
your bowl of eggs, impossible to catch.
On your canvas, the past and future
reel. Where are your muscles? You're no
rooster, though you're done up like a dandy,
pink rose in your lapel, curls like a girl's.
Of course you're torn. Your village
doesn't even know what country it's in.
Marc Chagall, you schmuck, you must pick,
you must choose, or the paint will harden
in the tube. Then you're stuck. It's 1971
in Marina del Rey. My father is smoking
a cigarette and sprinkling pepper on his eggs.
A baby is sneezing, and a woman is wiping
her eyes with the back of her hand.

Lake of Time

Shoulders back, prom girls. You are so lovely
and so unaware of what a difference
posture makes. Who taught you how to do that
to your eyes? You, your hair a chandelier
of braids or you, tugging your dress up or
down, your train dragging the grass, heels spiking
the damp ground, you, in cowboy boots and lace,
or tuxedoed, pompadoured—all of you
butterflies on a leaf, trembling because
the Grand March across this Montana golf
course lawn is cold in May, because the leaf
trembles, the branch, the tree, the earth—from here
on out, you're stuck on this unsteady thing,
so stand up straight—it's easier that way.

Letter from the Ant Queen

> The first thing [any new queen ant] does is to tear off her wings, which she never expects to use again now that she has made her marriage flight.
>
> —WILLIAM ATHERTON DUPUY, *OUR INSECT FRIENDS AND FOES*

Call it Cubist, the way memory deals your features
one by one—the white scar on your forearm,
the citron of your eyes. Or call it a failure of memory,

a bad hand, this scattering of the body through time,
this rended collage of you. Why can't I see your hands
when I can see the purple bleach spot on the leg

of your brown pants? Your collarbone. Your teeth.
Why can't I walk into you as I walked into our house—
the yellow living room, orange grit on the sills? I could still

go straight to the cupboard and take out the airplane
mug and the King of my Heart mug, or into the backyard,
pecans crunching in the crabgrass under my feet, garbage

lodged against the alley fence, a nest of white feathers
where the cats killed a dove. I can see my son crouched
on a spreading patch of bare ground, building stick bridges

for the harvester ants, pouring water down the entrance
to their colony to watch them swarm out, dragging
their drowned. Down there the queen can live twenty

years in darkness, licking her young like kittens. Is it
different for you, because I was a place you could enter?
I can still see the weathered boards of the porch,

the pots of flowers I sold when we left. I want to squeeze
the pink jaws of the snapdragons until their mouths open
and I hear what they have to say after all this time:

Remember me? I bloomed for you.
I still need you, contained here as I am.

The Repetitive Bird

Remember the day we walked along
the river and found a folded sheet
of paper sealed in a plastic bag, a page
from the *Personal Realities* section
of *The Urantia Book*, which we had
to Google? *Technical analysis does*
not reveal what a person or a thing
can do. In the left margin, a bullseye:
the *spirit nucleus*. Who doesn't need
a *Thought Adjustor, a Mystery*
Monitor? In the bar, the band plays
"Love the One You're With"—an awful
song, but will I ever stop looking around
to see how many lives I might have?
They play it as a ballad, *molto ritardando*,
for the bachelorettes and the ranchers
and one cute hippie kid, barely twenty-one,
dancing with a woman my age in an ugly
sweater who must be his mother. Maybe
I'll leave everyone eventually. Of course
I will. Remember the Repetitive Bird?
Like the beginning of Beethoven's
5th, with one fewer note—*dum da dum,*
dum da dum. Molto ritardando, over
and over at civil dawn, the blue hour,
while we lay in something close to
savasana, the cabin quiet, mice asleep.
The only sixth sense is proprioception.
I know well, now, where my body is,

how it's positioned and balanced, how
hard or gently to grasp. Unless you're
drunk, it's easy. Even plants can do it.
That bird could be a golden-crowned
sparrow in its non-breeding range. Those
opening notes—most likely, for Beethoven,
the song of the yellowhammer, not fate
hammering the door. You held me so
lightly I couldn't feel your hands at all.
To get fully into the body is to get out
of the body, to enter yoga nidra, dream
yoga, maybe even the trance bardo.
That day at the river, we found a little
charm—three square beads that spelled
the name Sam, short for Samantha,
probably, in blue and pink letters, but I
read it then, and now, upside down,
as *mas*, *mas*, the more I've always wanted.

Self-Portrait on Valentine's Day

Table for three at the China Buffet, where she and the children
eat spinach with cheese sauce, crab legs fished from a pot
of cloudy water, and those oil-soaked holeless doughnuts
her older son likes, the one watching YouTube on his phone
as the younger one slips a marinated bean into his brother's soda—

Her last crab leg dinner ended in an argument so intense
she walked five blocks in ten degrees in peep-toe heels,
and each winter since, her toes turn grey and swell and ache.
Feet in the stirrups, she asked, and her gynecologist confirmed—
like some STDs, frostbite lasts forever. This day like the double

videos her son watches—Beastie Boys on half the screen, Darth
Vader on the other. On one side, her lover has brought roses,
and she wears a red silk dress and Roxy Music's "More Than This"
plays as birds land on her outstretched hands, and she feels
transcendent—but on the other side, her wings are waterlogged,

body numb, like the girl on the Internet who can't feel pain,
whose family watched her bite the tip of her finger off,
or the college kid who locked himself out, barefoot and drunk,
and lost half of each foot, or like the roses in the dumpster.
Such a waste—encased in ice, they won't be ruined until they thaw.

Pointillist Self-Portrait

At the table next to mine, the volume
of the argument about upcycling lingerie
rises. Outside it's eight degrees
and the solstice sun glares. How can
anything so low cast so much light—
ice swirls like handfuls of glitter
tossed. The man says, *I understand*
if you don't want to be part of it,
but it's clear he's angry. I've never
worn a corset, but the Internet offers
plenty of advice. From the woman
with the alarming seventeen-inch waist,
The great advantage of permanent
corset-wearing is that your body
does not ever again have to adjust
to new circumstances—as though
she's trying to squeeze herself in two,
divide head from body, mouth from
bowels, heart from genitals. Yes.
That might be nice. I come from
the South, where a man should be
able to circle a woman's waist
with his hands. My mother used to
write songs and sing them to me—
one began *My fellow brings me poinsettias,*
and it was not very good, maybe
because poinsettias keep their sexual
parts hidden, although in the South
they grow outdoors year-round.

When our neighbor went to jail,
we adopted her cat Maxy, a big
Maine Coon, and my son made a trail
of heart-shaped treats from the kitchen
to his room, and we let Maxy out,
because he wanted to go, and he came
back at first and then didn't. Some things
I don't have to try to know I won't like—
the Gravitron, or winter camping,
piles of ice like a bulldozed igloo.
And *you should know*, the woman says,
maybe about the corset, but maybe not—
it's not a suffering-through thing.

Mr. No More Cowboy Hat

When's the last time anyone called you
magnificent? Try never. On the edge of absurd,
those m-words—if he had called your voice
mellifluous, you would've laughed. But how
not to be charmed by a man wearing
a cowboy hat in a swimming pool at night
who slides his hand up your leg from ankle
to thigh and calls you *magnificent*? But
was that the last night ever, with that hat?
Now it's glasses and hoodies—now it's
compliments just state the obvious. And
what happens when there's some practical
problem—you're out of firewood and it's twenty
degrees and Mr. No More Cowboy Hat has
a date with deep depression or Sunday
football, so you split and load by yourself—
fingers numb in splinter-covered gloves,
tears pricking your eyes like the prick
of a needle in a fairy tale that means
something's going to change or freeze
forever. You wish he would cry—that you
could dig up his tears from however deeply
they're buried and juice them, like carrots.
Is it empathy or fury that makes you imagine
pushing them one by one into some kind of
emotion-juicer that is, you have to admit,
something like a vagina, though you've
never been that naïve. Still, you imagine
feeding them into a machine that both is

and is not your body, petrified tears
like the tusks of a woolly mammoth.
Like the whole mammoth, excavated
from eons of ice. Where in the body
would you find them, stuck like kidney
stones or salivary stones? And how to
harvest them—those little daggers—
a shiv or a shank hidden in a boot or belt
or sock? When he said he's never lonely,
you felt like you do when a student turns in
a clearly plagiarized paper. If it's possible
to plagiarize the absence of loneliness.
Which it is, though not convincingly, or why
all those hours on Facebook, all those selfies
in the hat, before he stopped wearing it?

Letter from the Queen of the Crows

Every crow on the block made sure we couldn't
miss it—the fledgling under the rosebush, the whole
crow family shrieking and swooping overhead.
Half-grown, it bobbed and weaved across the grass,
opened its beak in a soundless caw, stretched
its sparse wings and hopped to the handlebar
of Scotty's bike, dancing the log roll as the plastic
slipped under its feet. Scotty asked again if animals
get married, but what he meant was, do they make
babies like people do? Old enough to know
better, he insists on saying *brung* instead
of *brought*

                    and you know how I feel
about the *dirty U*, vowel of *fuck* and *cunt*—the *uh*,
the grunt of lust. Note that I said *lust* and not *desire*.
So I brung the cats in the house. And of desire, note
that I am silent, except to say that as I watched it
struggle against the fence—the human blue
of its gaze, three-pronged talons scraping the dirt
like garden forks—I couldn't tell the difference
between terror and disregard. Did it think I meant
to feed or kill it? Impossible eye to read, under elms
that leaf so late they look dead most of spring,
then flower and drop flat papery fruit that drifts
like snow, clogs the gutters and sprouts—beautiful
word, *samara*—ivory wing for carrying seeds away.

Remember What You Said About Women

Remember what you said about women,
how *they carry around their little bag*
of poo, like a Crown Royal bag containing
every grievance they can't forgive. Up
Deer Creek on your friend Bob's property,
we cut firewood—gunshots from the rifle
range so constant the horses didn't startle.
In the stable, someone had put all the shit
from the barn cats into a bag labeled Purina
Apple and Oat Treats. I told my son
to reach in and get some for the horses.
Even when he said, more than once,
they weren't horse treats, I insisted until
he pulled a piece of cat shit out of the bag,
hard gray lumps linked by hair or grass,
like beads on a string, like bullets or DNA
or anal beads that literally spent time
up someone's ass. Only then, I believed him.
And he, knowing all along, close to tears,
had to hold dried cat shit to show me.
How many other moments like that, when
something that should have been good
went bad because I didn't see what was
in front of me. Because I was so afraid
of being alone I couldn't tell the difference
between cat shit and little heart-shaped
apple-oat cakes. Especially if some man
like you told me cat shit was a treat.
It's not *bringing up all that old shit*—

it's *identifying a pattern*, how one thing
is like another is like another. Beads
on a string. At the horse property, a spring
pours from a pipe in the side of a hill
like the coldest words possible. It's lovely
now though, that muddy green place
where water spills and spills and flows out
until the dirt can absorb it, and the planted
bulbs of tulip and hyacinth give way
to scrubby grass and knapweed and the ground
is finally thawed enough to bury the dead.

Lake of Hope

Like those playa lakes in Texas, shallow mudflats
it seems wrong to call the lovely word *ephemeral*—
unswimable, terminal, they're going nowhere
or drying up, frozen around the edge in low
January light. It's hard to care much what will happen
to the world since my son is gone. I am mostly all
I can think of. It's called *ambiguous grief*, this mourning
for the living, this loss that circles like thousands
of geese, then lands, obscuring the water.
Or like a quarry, or *I'm sorry, I'm sorry*—
like the pit in Butte, forty billion poison gallons
the geese see from air and mistake for a safe place.

Resident Ghost

I don't mean he was still there after twenty years,
slumped at the bottom of the basement stairs,
the hole in his chest still blooming. Why
would he have meant me harm in those nine
months I lived where he died? What I believe
is what remained remained as ozone after
lightning strikes, a disturbance, not a charge.
No cost to me or him, except my fear—
gestating, unattached. I reached into the tangled
snap pea vines and heard a crackle as my hand
broke one long thread of web—the spider
a tan lump on a tan leaf, pulsing. At night,
breath seemed to rise from the diamond-shaped
holes of the metal grate, nothing below
but a tight corner, the furnace, the washer
and dryer—no bloodstains on concrete, no echo
of screams. I wrapped the baby in fleece
and stood in the yard, under the silver maple—
hunting season, my husband gone, one deer
already hanging. There was no one I could ask.
And what would I have said? I couldn't
live there—flowers on the table, clean
Berber carpet, the cradle and the bed.

The Texan

The most interesting thing about him:
Antarctic Specially Protected Area 165,
named for his uncle. Stationed on the real
earth, he studied satellite geodesy—
the geoid, an idealized globe without
topography, without winds or tides.
The earth tranquilized. Geodesy is not
The Odyssey, though he must have been
on one. Was he more like Frankenstein
or Frankenstein's creature, crossing
the polar ice? As in love, the pursued
has the power. Doesn't it matter,
though, whether power is taken or given?
Which kind of creature was The Texan?
Which kind am I? What his uncle pursued
had nothing to do with love or revenge
or seals or Adelie penguins. No fur,
no feathers, just ice and rock, something
orbital. A geoid is not a geode, though
The Texan hoped to be both, hoped I'd
look past his ordinary exterior, crack
him open to find sparkling druze
or amethyst shards. I tried, but inside
more slush than mineral. He could've
been sharper, less fragile, more like real
crystal, less willing, like sugar or salt,
to dissolve. He should've known
it would hurt, being shattered. Gone
twenty years, Odysseus was no one's

ideal man—I wouldn't have waited.
For The Texan, I couldn't even wait
a month—out of love by the time he
arrived, I sent him back like misaddressed
mail. But was it all my fault? He thought
what women liked was to be bent
into improbable angles, to have their
flexibility measured and put to use.
He called this *the normal way*, found
me deficient for desiring anything else.
And he ordered more food than we could
eat—I wanted a man who'd split
an omelet, admit to being poor. Poor
Texan, whatever happened to him?
His brother got married; his father
lost an election. But other than that,
some people really have no Internet
presence—it's like they don't exist.
They just drink Diet Pepsi all day
and listen to bad music. I should have
known when I told him I didn't like
Led Zeppelin—*Then what do you*
listen to during sex? he said.

Self-Portrait in Downtown Missoula

Three Travelers recline on the corner
in late-August smoke. They're like the sun,
these men with brick-colored skin
and dreaded hair—don't look directly
at them. Their two dogs quiver on one
tattered rope, all head, a pair of deadly
tadpoles. In a mercurochrome glaze,
the sun looks more like Mars, the grass
a desiccated russet. Over the mountain,
retardant streams from a plane in a sudden
red gush. The night my husband drove us
off a cliff, eighty feet down to the ice
at the edge of the river, I went up
on a bodyboard, clinging to a boy
my husband flagged down on the highway.
The nurse kept asking if I knew Madeline DeFrees—
the nun who became a poet. So long ago,
that haze of morphine, my X-ray glowing
on the wall, shoulder splintered like a spring
tree under snow. When the doctor asked
what I wanted to use my arm *for*,
I couldn't imagine my body other than
an immaculate wholeness I had lost.
On the curb at the men's feet, a box
of doughnuts sits open, studded with flies.
Maybe they're selling them, or someone
gave them a sweetness they refused.
So long ago, my own renunciation.
I was a nun too then, in my way.

Namaste

That word you said—*incorrigible*—a brag
from a boy pretending to apologize for his
sexual appetite while showing off his vocabulary.
A Holden Caulfield kind of word. Hot in high
school but annoying now, that boy who never
grew up—forgivable only if you're fictional.
But I don't want to keep going, because once
I make fun of you in a poem, it's all over.
Even if you don't get mad, you'll get stuck
there, and I'm tired of boys who get stuck,
who die or sleep in a chair in their mother's
basement with the TV on and crumbs in their
beard. That's not you. How about *corrugated*
instead, a fine word for cardboard or the fiberglass
roof my son climbed onto to retrieve the Frisbee
and got splinters in his hands. Have I told you
the thing he and I used to say in the car—
You're Lester Schwab. No, you're Lester Schwab,
back and forth like the worst insult ever, while
he narrated the social life of Lester and his wife
Bertha and that other couple, Eugene and Ethel,
that they play—*what's that game old people
play, mom?*—bridge with on Friday nights.
You know I can't talk about lost boys without
talking about my son. Or about Pete, whom
we're both sick of. From him, I'm taking some
things back. I'll start with those two songs—
all the nights he came home at 2:00 or 3:00 or 4:00 a.m.
and sat on the couch listening to a sped-up

version of Springsteen's "I'm On Fire" sung by
a woman who probably looked like a Suicide Girl,
all tattoos and black bangs, probably someone
he knew, because I couldn't find that version
anywhere, and it was good, that was the thing—
she was on fire and he was on fire and I was
on fire, half with the need for him to turn it off
so I could sleep and get up at 6:00 and go to work
and half with jealousy, because if you know me
at all, which you do, you know I wanted him
no matter what, and you know, too, how badly
I wanted to be the one singing. Which brings me
to the other song, that time in Chicago at his mother's
house when Melissa Minnix posted to Facebook
a video of her singing "Angel from Montgomery"—
a few months of guitar lessons and a half-decent
smoky voice, and I didn't even like the song
but I was on fire for her courage, and he picked
that moment to tell me that when we lived
in Lubbock and I thought he was fucking her
and he said he wasn't, he was. Watching
her strum along in her cute red cowboy boots,
I thought of how he made fun of the way
I said her name, as if I wanted to hiss or spit,
as if I were saying *minx*, sleek and expensive,
or *menace*, which I thought she was, though she
likely had no idea I existed, and she was just
another artsy single mom, a yoga teacher
or massage therapist—pretty and good at touching
people, the same woman he always chose,
except me, more likely to throw tires across
a gym than whisper *namaste* with my palms
pressed together, but maybe it's time I did.

SOURCE ACKNOWLEDGMENTS

The American Journal of Poetry: "I Don't Require Durability in a Swan"
A Poetry Congeries: "Red-Winged Blackbirds," "Asked to Imagine the Death of my Son"
Atticus Review: "Ice Apples"
Bennington Review: "The Petroleum Club"
The Carolina Quarterly: "When Frankenstein Chased His Creature across the Ice," "Postcolonial Melancholia"
Evergreen: Fairy Tales, Essays, and Fables from the Dark Northwest: "Self-Portrait as a Stranger," "Resident Ghost"
Gulf Coast: "The Puppy and Kitten Channel"
Iron Horse Literary Review: "Self-Portrait with Northern Lights," "Pointillist Self-Portrait," "Self-Portrait in Downtown Missoula"
New Ohio Review: "The Men at Snowbowl Teaching Their Daughters to Ski," "Free Association"
Poetry Northwest: "Antillia," "Mr. No More Cowboy Hat"
Talking River: "Lake of Delight," "Lake of Death," "Sea of Desire," "Lake of Hope"
32 *Poems*: "Self-Portrait with Seven Fingers"
River Styx: "What Are We Going to Turn Into?"
Southern Humanities Review: "Self-Portrait on Valentine's Day," "Self-Portrait Playing Tennis,"
Willow Springs: "The Repetitive Bird"

BACKWATERS PRIZE IN POETRY

2022	Laura Reece Hogan, *Butterfly Nebula*
	Honorable Mention: Henrietta Goodman, *Antillia*
2021	Laura Bylenok, *Living Room*
	Honorable Mention: Sophie Klahr, *Two Open Doors in a Field*
2020	Nathaniel Perry, *Long Rules: An Essay in Verse*
	Honorable Mention: Amy Haddad, *An Otherwise Healthy Woman*
2019	Jennifer K. Sweeney, *Foxlogic, Fireweed*
	Honorable Mention: Indigo Moor, *Everybody's Jonesin' for Something*
2018	John Sibley Williams, *Skin Memory*
2017	Benjamín Naka-Hasebe Kingsley, *Not Your Mama's Melting Pot*
2016	Mary Jo Thompson, *Stunt Heart*
2015	Kim Garcia, *DRONE*
2014	Katharine Whitcomb, *The Daughter's Almanac*
2013	Zeina Hashem Beck, *To Live in Autumn*
2012	Susan Elbe, *The Map of What Happened*
2004	Aaron Anstett, *No Accident*
2003	Michelle Gillett, *Blinding the Goldfinches*
2002	Ginny MacKenzie, *Skipstone*
2001	Susan Firer, *The Laugh We Make When We Fall*
2000	David Staudt, *The Gifts and the Thefts*
1999	Sally Allen McNall, *Rescue*
1998	Kevin Griffith, *Paradise Refunded*

The Backwaters Prize in Poetry was suspended from 2005 to 2011.

Printed in the USA
CPSIA information can be obtained
at www.ICGtesting.com
CBHW031249060524
8103CB00001B/60

9 781496 236081